Start, Ope
Grow Your Personal
Training Business

Everything You Need to Know to Get Started for Low Cost as a Personal Fitness Professional

Chris Lutz

Master Trainer

DEDICATION

I dedicate this book to all of my fitness entrepreneur friends and supporters, my Mom and Dad for supporting me and giving me a great start in life.

CONTENTS

FOREWORD

The personal training profession, like many other professions, it is relatively simple to get into, looks easy to make a lot of money but the reality is there are only a few who can make a good living doing it. My good friend, Chris Lutz, owner and founder of S.P.A.R.T.A. - Sports Performance and Resistance Training Association, has put together a comprehensive step by step process to help those who are genuinely interested in making personal training a profession and not just a hobby. This step-by-step approach will take you through the planning stages of getting the business started with the basics of a business plan through to hiring and staffing a personal training business. Chris simplifies the forgotten step in most personal training certification, the sales process. In this book Chris explains simple steps to follow in sales process from prospecting for potential clients to networking and building the brand of the business to finally setting up a recurring EFT billing system so collecting money becomes a breeze.

These are the exact systems and skills I work hard at teaching new trainers every day. Take the step by step approach described in this and apply it to your personal training business and you can save years of trial and error and start your way to a successful personal training business.

Like any other business or successful venture, one needs to plan. Success is not easy, but the process can be fun and very rewarding.

Dwayne Wimmer
Owner
Vertex Fitness Personal Training Studio
Philadelphia, PA

ACKNOWLEDGMENTS

This book would not have been possible without the endless love, support, and encouragement from Rachel Wright, Larry Lutz, Ruth Lutz, Dwayne Wimmer, Jennifer Payette, Franny Goodrich, and all of our certified trainers and members.

A special thanks to Indra Books for compiling much of this information for us early on and Jennifer Abernethy for inspiring the hard copy idea for this book.

1 WHY PERSONAL TRAINING?

Personal fitness training isn't a new field. It's becoming less and less thought of as a luxury service. There are many niches and populations of people you can serve in your area. And with the aging population of baby boomers, you stand to have a readily available market for your services.

First of all, it will probably have to be something that you're interested in and passionate about. If not, it probably won't work no matter what business it is. Realize that you'll have even more work to do in addition to regular technical training of clients. You'll need to be proficient with sales, marketing, prospecting, networking, and maybe even hiring and firing of staff and employees. There is a lot more to running a personal training business than just the training. That's the reality of it. I have more of an interest in running a quality and efficient business. I just to happen to have built up good technical training skills too. For most people, it is the reverse. But, that's not to say that if you lack experience in those other things you can't get into the field. There aren't too many reference books on the subject like this. Many of us get into business and fly by the seat of our pants and learn as we go. Sometimes they are some hard lessons, but the point was that we took action and did it and persevered through the mistakes.

Luckily, the field of personal training is still relatively easy to get into. There are low barriers to entry, low or no costs, and virtually no regulation depending on the state in which you live. If you have an interest in it, it can be a great way to make extra money or have a nice paying career if you're able to fill your schedule with high paying clients. It's a fairly high ticket item still usually ranging anywhere from $60-$150 per hour. We have charged at several price points within that range and done quite well. You can too. There are elements of art and science to it. The science is relatively easy and doesn't take long to learn how to prescribe programs for certain kinds of clients. The art part comes with more experience and likely can't be taught. Most of it centers around your ability to think critically and adapt to situations presented by clients. Your ability to foster and cultivate positive relationships with clients will also feed into the art side of this field.

Typically, if you have a day job or if you're still in school as a college student, a part time job as a trainer can serve you well. You'll make a high amount of money per time and clients usually tend to be able to make appointments before and after work saving the middle of your day for your other job or classes. In fact, that's how I worked my way through college. Other benefits include not needing to have a brick and mortar facility. You can travel to client's homes or work places. You can rent or contract with larger facilities saving you thousands in startup costs. It is far more about the knowledge you can acquire and the service you can deliver rather than the tangible assets you bring to the table.

Now, it isn't always rosy. There are some drawbacks. The hours can be long and start in the early morning and go late into the evening. The good thing is, you can make your own hours if you're self-employed as long as you're still able to serve clients at those times. Knowing all of that, if you still have interest and think it's something you'd like to pursue, let's get started and explore what you need to succeed.

Certification and Education:

You'll need a certification and it could possibly help reduce your insurance costs. We recommend our own evidence based Training certification levels 1-3. It is a turnkey system of principles that will help you quickly learn the skills needed to prescribe safe, effective, and efficient exercise routines to your clients.

Keep in mind that certification is only the lowest rung of the ladder. There is no substitute for experience or mentoring. As far as formal education goes, it might be even more beneficial for you to obtain undergraduate degrees in business or maybe even graduate degrees in physical therapy. If you ever wanted to choose to open a clinical facility, your options would broaden quite a bit with the ability to take on patients whose insurance plans will pay for their treatments. This population of people could roll right into regular clients once therapeutic goals have been met or insurance runs out. Currently, many schools, and states now require, a 3 year doctorate in physical therapy to be licensed. It's something to think about and weigh the pros and cons. Obviously, you'll have more education expenses, and possibly lots of student debt, before you ever get to starting your business. But, go with what you feel and can reasonably forecast will be right for the vision of your business.

ACE, ACSM, NSCA, and NASM are some of the larger and more popular certifying organizations. They all have different methodologies and agendas. There are some 500 other certifying bodies in the country creating a very diluted marketplace. But, like I said earlier, you'll have to do some research and decide what is right for the scope of your business. Going forward, self-education is going to be key. One thing that the majority of certification organizations are missing is the business component which is the purpose of the creation of this book and our organization overall.

Incorporation:

Make sure to incorporate in your state by going to your state corporation commission or equivalent office. An LLC will most likely be the right choice for a single member personal trainer company, but check with your attorney or accountant to be sure. Make sure to obtain a local county or town business license.

You'll need to call the IRS and obtain an EIN (employer identification number). This is like your business' social security number. You'll need it to open your business bank account later. Be sure to obtain any trademarks either state or national that might be pertinent to your business logo, slogan, etc.

Naming your business. You'll want to name your business something that is descriptive of what you do or offer and reflects your personal brand. The same is true for your logo design. To operate under a different business name or a shortened one (like S.P.A.R.T.A.) you can file a simple DBA, Doing Business As, form with your state corporation commission. You may need to do this so that you do not have to use the LLC at the end of your name if you chose to incorporate as a limited liability company.

Taxes:

Consult with your accountant and set up all necessary federal and state tax accounts. Some accountants will come in one day per week and take care of your transactions for the week all in one shot. Better yet, they can monitor your transactions and work with you virtually. As a matter of fact, I've never even met our bookkeeper in person Sometimes you can find a personal assistant or concierge that can do bookkeeping for you. If you have employees, there will be further accounts to set up. Paying your estimated taxes on a quarterly basis will most likely be easiest and economical.

Bank Account:

Go to your favorite local bank (they aren't that much different) and set up a business checking account and merchant services to accept credit cards and, most importantly, EFT (electronic funds transfer) or ARB (automatic recurring billing). Preferably go to one where you have a contact working there. Sometimes a local credit union can be a good option too and maybe better in some instances than the larger banks. See if you can set up a business line of credit at that visit as well for a little extra cushion in the future. Based on our experience, credit unions may not be as good as dealing with small business as some other commercial banks are, but it's worth looking into first. Setting up this account is where you will need the EIN number you get from the IRS.

Up until this point, you may not have much money to open the account with. That's ok too. We used the revenue from our first client to open our account. She paid us with a check and we deposited it soon thereafter.

If you're really bootstrapping, you may be able to make use of some online resources early on like Paypal or maybe even Google Checkout. Paypal has a virtual terminal option and a subscription feature for recurring billing of your clients. More on that later. Additionally, they have merchant services like the web code for buttons you can simply cut and paste into your website as you develop it.

Legal:

If you can afford it, find an attorney and pay him a retainer to become a client when legal issues arise. Or at the very least, create a list of people you could call when legal issues come up. Additionally, some services like Pre-paid Legal or maybe even Legal Zoom can offer some peace of mind and help solve smaller more routine legal issues should they arise.

Insurance:

You'll need personal liability and business insurance. Check with a local independent insurance agent or your bank can possibly offer one of these programs.

Philadelphia Insurance Companies is the primary provider of policies for fitness professionals. It's called Fitness Instructor and Personal Trainer Insurance. You can go right to their website to apply.

Along the same lines as an insurance policy, you'll want to be CPR/AED certified. AED stands for Automatic External Defibrillator. These are available in many facilities now for quick response in the event of cardiac emergencies. You'll want to be certified in both if you can as well as CPR for children and first aid. As long as you act as a prudent person would and within the scope of your training, no harm can come to you if you were to intervene in a situation. It won't hurt and you'll likely be able to do it all at the same time.

2 PERSONAL TRAINER BUSINESS PLAN

The Personal Trainer Business Plan Worksheet

Description of business
(Summary):_____
_____
_____
_____
_____

Vision:_____
_____
_____
_____

Mission
Statement:_____
_____
_____
_____

Unique Selling
Proposition:_____
_____

_____
_____
_____
_____

Detailed Marketing
Strategy:_____
_____
_____
_____
_____
_____
_____
_____
_____
_____
_____

What are Your Revenue
Channels:_____
_____
_____
_____
_____
_____

Management
Team:_____
_____
_____
_____
_____

Who is your
competition?:_____
_____

_____
_____
_____
_____

**Key Success
Strategies:**_____
_____
_____
_____
_____

**Top
Strengths:**_____
_____
_____
_____
_____

**Top
Weaknesses:**_____
_____
_____
_____
_____

**Top Risks to Your
Business:**_____
_____
_____
_____
_____

Financial assumptions:

Where will you secure funding
from:_____

_____
_____
_____
_____
_____

How Much do You Need Annually to Break
Even:_____

_____
_____

      Expected Expenses:_____
      Expected Revenues:_____

Annual Revenue Needed for Profitability_____
Ideal # of Clients _____
Revenue per Client _____
Retention rate _____

Expected Profit Increase Over First
Year:_____

Niche Markets You Will
Serve:_____

_____
_____
_____
_____
_____

Growth
Strategy:_____

_____
_____

_____

_____

_____

Marketing Strategy
Overview:_____

_____

_____

_____

_____

_____

Exit
Strategy:_____

_____

_____

_____

Action Items for
Implementation:_____

_____

_____

_____

_____

_____

3 SALES-HOW TO SET UP ARB IN YOUR PERSONAL TRAINING BUSINESS

A better way to bill and retain your clients and avoid "selling". It's no secret; most personal trainers hate to sell. They hate to sell themselves and they hate to sell their services. That's fine, a lot of people have a hard time pricing themselves and that gets better with more experience as an entrepreneur. But, if you hate doing it, don't put yourself in a position where you are forced to do it over and over again. What am I talking about?

EFT or ARB. EFT is electronic funds transfer, or as my bank calls it, automatic recurring billing. We are fortunate to be in an industry where typically, your services are paid for ahead of time. That's great. You don't have to bill your clients after the fact and constantly chase down up to 50% of them to get paid for what you have already performed. So, we are a step ahead on that one.

Now why do most trainers continue to sell single sessions or packages of 10, 20 or more sessions? What happens at the end of that 10 or 20? You are in a position where most of the value of your clients comes from repeat business. Selling a fixed number of sessions implies that they will stop at some point. Not what you want!! You want them to fall in love with you and not be able to exercise without you.

Every time you come to an end of a package, you have to resell them on another package. If they bought a big one up front, how are you going to convince them to buy a big one again? If they see that big dollar amount, they may want to go for the smaller package this time. How are you going to top your original sales pitch to get them to sign up the first time? Worst of all, they may just take it as an opportunity to "take a break" or stop altogether. Does this sound familiar? Wouldn't it be better if you could have a better chance at retaining these people, more predictable and reliable income, and not have to resell people every time they complete their package with you? The fact is, there is.

Just take a look at what your own gym does to you. They sign you up with an advance (initiation fee), slowly dribble a recurring monthly fee out of your account...automatically. If they are smart, they locked you into a long term deal like a year or more. Some places will lock you in for 3 years. Those days may be gone for a while. I like to advertise and use as a selling point, month to month agreements, but that's because I know the likelihood of someone quitting after only the first month or two is low. It makes them feel comfortable not having to "commit" to something too big or for too long. The point is that the system is automatic, just like a gym membership. Think of what you are selling as a personal training membership. Here's how we have done it.

You'll need a business bank account with your EIN number. You can obtain that from the IRS after you are a legal business entity. Once you have your business bank account, ask about their merchant services and the ability to take credit cards. My bank uses a virtual terminal through authorize.net. Even other services like Paypal now have a business account and virtual terminal option to make things easy. The point is to find a payment processor that will allow you to take and process credit cards automatically. There will likely be a very small transaction fee and something like 2-3% of the total transaction. And possibly the more volume of transactions you do, the lower your rate will be. It can look like a lot when your statement comes, especially for American Express cards, but with such a high priced service, we should be able to maintain relatively high margins to allow for this. Plus, NOT having the headaches of chasing people down, keeping track of sessions, getting bad checks, etc. makes up for the relatively small costs of processing credit cards and doing it automatically.

The crucial feature of this system is the ability to set up recurring payments on a monthly basis automatically. So for every new client I see, I sell them on one of our options, usually either 2 or 3 times per week (it's cheaper per session the more frequent they workout). From here on out, it is just a monthly membership. You can choose to charge them an initiation fee if you like or not. If not, make sure you note that to them so they know how much they are saving. If you own a facility, I would charge them a small one. Let's say they want to train 2 times a week at $60/session. You'll read more about pricing your service later on in the operations chapter. That's $480/month. Let's make it look more marketable and call it $479/month. That's it. You enter that into your system open ended with no end date and let it roll until they need to stop, if they need to. I've had clients for the better part of a decade on this system and I've never stopped it.

You can tell them that twice per week is 8 workouts a month based on a 4 week month. Some months have 5 weeks so they may get 9 or 10 workouts, but only pay for 8. That's a plus for them. Or if they happen to take a week off out of 3 months, there's no penalty. That's another plus for them. Over the course of a year, you are actually giving them a full month for FREE if they are consistent (52 weeks in a year, but you only charge for 48). Another plus for them. Actually, due to sickness and vacation, they probably will end up taking that month off, but the point is that you are over delivering and accounting for things that may arise. This way they aren't paying for something that they aren't using like a traditional gym membership. If they need to take more time than that, then you can have them do make up sessions into the next month or simply adjust next month's payment amount. Some programs will let you skip a month or stop the subscription and restart it later. It's very easy to do without having to keep asking them to write big checks or give you their credit card over and over again. The more they feel like they are repeatedly paying you, the more they may consider cutting it out eventually. You want to remove that emotional action from your dealings with them so they see the transaction later on their credit card statement and it's just another bill coming from someone else, not you!!

Let's compare this to the same rate per session of $60 and you sold them 48 sessions that will last 6 months. The total for that package would be $2880. That's a lot to plunk down all in one shot for most people. That's a down payment on a sweet new car! Why would they want to waste that on PT? Good question. Many wouldn't. Now let's say you come to the end of that package. What is the likelihood that you will get a renewal for that amount again in a quick 6 months especially in a down economy when few people have much cash lying around? Maybe not the best chance. If you have this person on ARB, they will probably just blow right past that 6 month mark and you would not have to "resell" them again to keep working with you. You'd get more out of them, they are more consistent and get better results. In the long run, you are more likely to realize the true lifetime value of the client by increasing your retention by charging lower monthly fees.

There are a few different ways you can work this scenario, but above all else, do it monthly, and make it automatic. It also keeps the client more accountable by having their sessions attached to time instead of having someone stretch out 48 sessions over two years. That isn't helping anybody. This system will weed out those people as well so that you can focus on the more committed clients. For added stability and predictability, pro-rate your client's first month and start their next month on either the 1st or the 15th of the month, whichever is closest to their sign up date. This way you won't have unpredictability by having nothing coming in for 8 days and then $10,000 in one day. It will even out your cash flow and you should know exactly what is coming in twice per month. It will help with your cash flow to pay your own bills. And it should help you with your projections based on your monthly goal of new clients to acquire. Simply add the number of new clients and the resulting revenue to the monthly totals to find what you need to reach your monthly goals. It is a little utilized system, but the best in terms of what we have seen to sell and retain the clients that you worked hard to get.

Lutz

4 PERSONAL TRAINER MARKETING PLAN

The Personal Trainer Marketing Plan

What are your marketing objectives?

Market Research: (Are there people even willing to buy what you're offering and at what price?)_____
_____
_____

Branding:_____
_____
_____
_____

Repeat Business:
_____
_____
_____

Market segmentation:

Who will you sell to?   (individuals, small businesses, corporations)?

_____

_____

_____

_____

What are your keys strategies for success?
(For your convenience, 16 sample ideas have been added for you).

Top ways to generate leads in your market.

1.   Create a referral program for incentive for your current clients to refer you more. FREE.

2.   Put simple free ads on craigslist, backpage, etc. daily. Use more than one category Advertise a FREE consultation or a FREE eBook they can receive for emailing you back. Continue to follow up with your inquiries. FREE.

3.   Put your business cards and brochures up in grocery stores or coffee houses with community bulletin boards.   Use www.vistaprint.com to produce them. FREE or very low cost.

4.   Write a FREE eBook or report. Put it on your website for download in exchange for their email address. FREE.

5.   Have a website. $20/year.

6.   Start a blog. Go to www.wordpress.com and set one up. Put up content rich info at least once a week for your niche. FREE.

7.   Collect emails for your email list to market to. Send out a content rich newsletter twice a month. FREE. You can use outlook distribution list if you have about 30 clients or under, but you can graduate to a better newsletter service as you grow. www.aweber.com costs about $19/month.

8.   Call your old clients that have stopped and try to get them back in with a special offer once per month. FREE.

9.   Give out gift cards to your clients to give to their friends for a FREE consultation and FREE workout. FREE.

10. Give out gift cards to your network of business associates to hand out to THEIR clients as gifts. FREE.

11. Go to chamber of commerce events and network. Meet new people every day. Join a business networking group. Go into it trying to pass leads and referrals first, then they will refer to you. ~$250-300/year.

12. If you are starting out, get a few friends or loose acquaintances or gym members that would like to train with you and train them for free so they look good, lose fat, and make sure they refer paying clients to you in return. FREE.

13. Put a box in similar businesses with a great offer if people put their business card in. Go to hair salons, tanning salons, bridal shop, spas, massage therapists, etc. Try to get a bunch of these out there. Offer something in return to the owners like referring your clients to them or giving them a discount or free training. FREE.

14. Prospect daily!! Use your scripts and call your contacts to dig up leads of people they know that may benefit from your service. You may need to make 10-30 calls/emails a day for new leads. FREE. Prospecting scripts provided for you in a later chapter.

15. Ask your current clients what they would like to see or what they think is missing or could be better that you could implement maybe as another revenue stream. FREE.

16. Get out and speak in public. Give a seminar or workshop. Look for joint venture partners to put on event or raise money for charitable cause. FREE.

   *Note: Most activities trainers do for marketing can be low or NO cost other than your own time or some bartering. Only pay for marketing efforts when you have the budget or have to.

If you choose to do paid advertising, a random ad in the newspaper or on radio or TV will likely be costly and not work. Smaller and less expensive options might be to advertise in your local community newsletters or newspapers. I know one of my friends and classmates from college, Christy, built a large chunk of her personal training business off of a $5 community newspaper ad. The long term value of 1 client alone plus all the referrals she received added up to be an exponential return on investment.

Sometimes, it will be good to combine these efforts or put them together in more of a multi-step process. It doesn't always work like this:

Expensive ad = tons of new leads = tons of new clients

More likely, you'll end up with nothing. You'll want a targeted ad to your demographic or niche. You might not include anything about signing up for personal training immediately in your ad. Your only goal might be to direct them to your website to get something for free like a fat loss eBook in exchange for their email. Now that you have their email with their permission, you can continue to market to them over the long term using your email marketing software in the form of your newsletter or other special offers. It might take a year before someone decides to actually call you for a real free consultation in person. It's just the long term nature of building a relationship and trust among your prospects for you and your business. But, that's totally worth it. If you can multiply that effect and gradually work them up the ladder to your premium service to buy something large from you at full price.

Guarantee:

Why should they trust you and why should they hire you now? Can you guarantee your service?

Example: You are a S.P.A.R.T.A. endorsed trainer. You represent the best in terms of SAFE, EFFECTIVE, and EFFICIENT personal training services in the industry.

_____
_____
_____

Positioning as an Expert:

I am the ONLY trainer that:

_____
_____
_____

Advertising:

(Small newspaper ads, direct mail post cards, pay per click Google and Facebook ads). What efforts would you include?

_____
_____
_____
_____

Networking:

Who are the professionals or businesses that you could set up a referral relationship, joint venture, or co-promote with?

_____
_____
_____

Sales Promotions:

What are incentives I could provide to my current clients? (Bring up during check ins, monthly assessments, referral program).

_____
_____
_____
_____

PR and Press: (special events, media relations)

What are events you could hold, attend, or sponsor? (News worthy event, contest, or charity event).

_____
_____
_____
_____

Social Media
Strategy:_____

_____
_____

More on Personal Trainer Marketing

If you do a good job and your clients are seeing positive results, you'll likely get the majority of your new business from word of mouth referrals. You'll obviously need to have a good working relationship with your clients to where they love you and are very attached to you while at the same time their friends are seeing the changes in them you are helping to make. But, word of mouth is an organic process. You don't want to sit around and passively wait for phone calls to come in. Is there a way you can expedite the process? Yes there is. Use this form below to gather potential new clients from your current crop of clients who are doing well.

Referral Systems

Give Your Friends The Gift of Fat Loss And Fitness Success!

Dear S.P.A.R.T.A. Client,

Just like any other business, we need new clients to grow. Of course we advertise, but a better idea would be to let a few of our best clients and business partners give away our services as free gifts to their friends.

So that's exactly what we're doing. And here's how it works:

1.   Who do you know that would like to start a fitness program or may need some help with their current plan? A friend, neighbor, a relative? Just jot down their name on the enclosed form and give it or send it back to us, or call our office with their information.

2.   We'll include a gift certificate with a FREE consultation and FREE workout.

It's something they can use to improve their health and fitness and you look good giving it to them as a gift! And if your friend does decide to take advantage of our fitness programs you will receive 2 FREE personal training sessions (a $140 value).

Just pick up the phone and give me a call at 703-XXX-XXXX to give us the name of your friend and we'll take care of the rest from there. Or if you prefer, simply fill out the referral form below and send it or bring it back to us.

Either way, your friend will receive a FREE consultation and workout. Plus, you get to look good by giving them a gift and earn free sessions and we get the opportunity to expand our business. That way everybody wins.

Thank you again for your continued support.

Sincerely,

Chris Lutz, BS, CPT, Master Trainer

Refer-A-Friend

Please complete the form below and mail to:
S.P.A.R.T.A.
Herndon, VA 20171

Who do you know who could benefit from a workout regimen with S.P.A.R.T.A.?

1.

Name _____

Address_____

City _____ State ____Zip_____

Phone_____Email_____

2.

Name _____

Address_____

City _____ State ____Zip_____

Phone_____Email_____

3.

Name _____

Address_____

City _____ State ____Zip_____

Phone_____Email_____

You can easily produce business cards, post cards, brochures and flyers cheaply from a company called Vistaprint. www.vistaprint.com. You can even send out direct mail campaigns and purchase mailing lists directly through their site. They've come a long way in the last few years and are a great, low cost resource for entrepreneurs of all kinds. You'll need all of these resources at one time or another especially in networking settings which you'll be attending.

Networking

Joining the local chamber of commerce, some say it's worth it, some say it's not. The good news is that you'll likely be one of, if not the ONLY, personal trainer at the events. I rarely see any other fitness businesses when I go and we live in the richest county in the nation, Loudoun County, VA. So our chamber is large. Naturally, the people that see you often at the events will just assume you are the authority on exercise in the area because they don't see any other trainers out networking. That may be because most trainers don't like to get out and do a lot of networking face to face, but it is crucial that you move out of your comfort zone if you hope to meet new people and drum up new prospects. Once you get the hang of it, these activities are actually quite fun. I've been a member for over 5 years of our's. There are other organizations besides local chambers that specialize in professional networking like Business Networking International (BNI) among others. It's been a good experience, but you need to have a strategy in order to be successful.

Generally, I try to go to as many events as I can. You'll have to make a choice as they do have costs associated with them. So going to a lot can really add up, but could be more than worth it too. For me, if I get 1 or 2 clients a year from chamber activities, it's worth it. Obviously, I'm shooting for more than that. The large breakfasts and after hours mixers are fun and fairly productive. Leadshare is the most productive for us. It's a name for a program which consists of smaller, but closer groups where members join to "share leads". You get exclusivity in the group as you'll be the only personal trainer. You meet twice a month for lunch or breakfast. Each member gets 30 seconds to stand and introduce themselves and give their elevator speech. You'll want to have a standard and scripted elevator speech and not just wing it. You'll sound a lot more professional and get the vital information out that you need to your fellow group members. If you don't have an elevator speech, go to www.15SecondPitch.com and it is a tool that will help you craft an effective one. I met my certified financial planner (no commission financial advisor) who is a member of my leadshare group. That was a good connection for me as he is one of only 300 or so fee only advisors in the country. We also work on several joint ventures together. If you have a newsletter, it is a good idea to get the people that you have met and have a good relationship with on the newsletter. Another way you can always stay front of mind with your business associates, partners, and prospects.

Your most successful conversions to clients will be qualified leads. In other words, if you run across someone who needs to sell a house, try to get permission for the realtor in the group to give them a call or email to discuss the options using his/her services. I RARELY convert referrals where someone just gave somebody my name and number, they rarely call. Try to get the person providing the service or product to get in touch with the prospect if they'll take it. If you do this, you'll be far ahead of the rest of the group.

There are other events especially during the days in the form of luncheons, and expos, etc. These may be more appropriate for a personal trainer's schedule as after work hours may be prime time for you to train clients. However, it is vital that you make time to get out and continuously network so that you continue to drive new prospective clients into your marketing funnel.

Making the Most of Your 1 on 1 Networking Meetings with Other Professionals

When you're out networking you'll likely be in a group or at some even with many people. It's possible to develop relationships and get more leads this way, but think of it as a process especially if you are a member of a networking group. You'll have to take it a step further and likely meet with other members and professionals in the area in a 1 on 1 meeting. This allows you to get to know them and their business better and vice versa. You can usually meet them for lunch somewhere neutral. Ideally, if you have a facility, you want to get them to meet you there. You can even offer to bring lunch in for them. But, the purpose is to get them in to see your place and what you do. But, before we get ahead of ourselves, you'll need to take a couple of steps BEFORE the meeting to maximize the potential value. It's easy for these meetings to just deteriorate into talking shop and not really getting anything out of it but wasted time and lunch. I've used the following steps to keep on track in meetings like this with other professionals. They always comment about how organized, professional, and valuable the meeting was. People will appreciate that and hold you in higher regard. Use these steps yourself in your networking endeavors to stay on track, be more professional, and make the most of it.

Usually a day or 2 before the meeting, send an email with a description of your target market and what kind of leads you are looking for to the person you will be meeting with. Be extremely simple and clear in your description. Be a giver!! The more you give, the more you get. Example:

"Dear Mrs. Smith,
I will see you tomorrow at Panera Leesburg 12pm. If you get a few minutes when you get home, reply to this email with a description of who you are looking for as referral leads and I'll try to bring a couple names to the meeting.

We are looking for more 1 on 1 training clients or small groups of 2-3 people for reduced rate training. Our target market is a middle aged person, most likely women, married, and dual income who live in or close to Ashburn. We also target business owners, busy professionals, and entrepreneurs, themselves as they are very busy and can benefit from our time efficient program. They would generally like to lose body fat, improve strength, shape, stamina, and improve certain health markers in a safe and time efficient program (30 mins). We've had very good success with managing diabetes, osteoporosis, and arthritis.

If there's anything else I could help bring to the table to help you, please let me know. Thank you."

At the meeting, stand and greet the person with a firm handshake. Review this simple outline to keep you on track, maximize your time, and get the most out of your meeting.

1.   Info about your businesses: Take turns offering some background and history on yourself and your business and how you got to where you are today. Focus on your current products or services you have available. But, keep it simple. Your core service you offer. Don't confuse them. You want them to remember you as the one who offers…XXX…in your local area.

2.   Target market: Specifically, let the other person know exactly what kind of lead or referral you are looking for and/or a description of your target market. The more descriptive the better. Also, let them know the best way to have a lead or referral contact you. Inform your colleague of your unique selling proposition. What makes you or your business better, cheaper, or different than your competitors?

3.   Possible leads: Ideally, if you have a name or 2 with you, have the person you are meeting with call the person who is the lead. You'll need to get their (the lead's) permission to have your colleague give them a call or email. This will be your highest probability of it becoming a closed transaction. Try to have them do the same for you. We RARELY convert leads where someone just told them to give us a call. They almost never call. You need to be proactive about it and try to get contact info for the lead they are giving you so that you can get in touch with them.

Follow up:

If you can't bring any leads to the meeting, don't stop there. Make a plan to reconnect with a phone call or email in 3-5 days after you've had some time to digest your colleague's information and you've been able to look through you contacts to see what a good match for them is. Follow this outline and you'll stay on track and it should only take 1 hour and no more. You'll greatly increase both of your chances for obtaining more leads from your efforts. And hopefully, it will turn into a long and lucrative relationship with your fellow professionals in your area.

Email Marketing

Email marketing can be a useful branch of your overall marketing to stay front of mind with current and past clients as well as potential prospects for the future. We recommend a resource which is relatively low cost like Aweber www.aweber.com or Constant Contact www.constantcontact.com. Both have easy to use templates to send out regular email newsletters and emails in between. Aweber will offer you easier production of web forms to place on your site for opt-ins as well as email list segmentation and good autoresponder series emails. Aweber started out more of the autoresponder software. Constant Contact started out more as the newsletter software. We use both in our business, but you'll likely want to pick one or the other for your purposes. If I had to really choose only one, I'd probably stick with Aweber.

Getting Medical Referrals

Below is a quick intro letter sample you can use to send out to medical professionals in your area to hopefully open up a conversation and eventually a referral relationship. Notice how I open with something I can do to help his practice first. And then I even went so far as to offer this professional a little more name recognition and status within our organization.

April 12th, 2010

Dear Dr. Johnson,

You may remember we spoke about a year ago with regard to our safe and effective high intensity training personal training program. Tina, Marc's wife, put us in touch. I just wanted to check in with you to see if there's anything I can do to help you with your practice. You have an excellent reputation. If I have other clients like Marc, can I just refer them straight to you or is there a better way to put them in contact with you?

Since you seem pretty knowledgeable about our methods already, I also wanted to take the opportunity to offer you a place on my medical advisory board. You'll get your name and contact information placed on our website under our medical tab and it doesn't come with any other responsibility to you other than maybe answering a tough question that we may have come up from a client every now and then. It's good exposure for you and another place your name will be out on the internet that potential patients can find.

I'd encourage you to take a look at our medical page at www.spartatraining.com/medical.php for more scientific information and about the populations we work with including post-rehab clients. If you'd like to talk more about the possibility of building this relationship with us, you can call me anytime at the number listed below. In fact, I'd like to come in and meet with you very briefly to give you a little more detail on what we do.

Thanks in advance for your time and I look forward to hearing from you soon.

Chris Lutz-Master Trainer

President of S.P.A.R.T.A.

www.spartatraining.com

703-XXX-XXX

Corporate Wellness Workshop Proposal Sample

S.P.A.R.T.A
Herndon, VA 20171

January 26, 2011

Cindy Smith/Leigh Jones-XYZ Company
Accounting

Dear Cindy/Leigh:

I enjoyed meeting with you the other day to discuss some corporate wellness options, specifically, educational exercise and nutrition workshops for your company. Corporate wellness programs are well established in many industries. With rising costs of employment, these types of programs can be vital to a company reducing its' risk and reducing its' long term costs associated with a large workforce that is becoming ever more unhealthy and out of shape. Creating a culture of health, fitness, and wellness is a very strong strategy when many other factors may be out of company control. Programs can be focused not only on keeping those who are healthy that way, but also those with chronic or pre-existing conditions a way to manage those conditions and reduce down time, sickness, and associated costs.

This correspondence outlines the complete scope of work you requested, including objectives, procedures, and identification of responsibilities.

OBJECTIVE

To implement an educational exercise and nutrition seminar/interactive workshop for the benefit of employees of XYZ Company. The workshop will be no cost to the company. It is purely an educational opportunity to further the health knowledge of its' employees to create a better work environment, a healthier workforce, and reduce company long term costs. The workshop will be approximately 1 hour in length and be divided up equally with 50% emphasis on the benefits and importance of safe, effective, and efficient regular exercise and 50% on simple and sound nutritional and weight management principles. The level of content should be appropriate to all attendees. Information and tools provided are something employees can put into practice immediately to improve their health, lives, and subsequent productivity at work.

SCOPE OF SERVICES

1. Procedures
   A. Plan an appropriate educational workshop for a company with 100+ employees.
   B. Prepare materials attendees will be using to determine their own individual health/nutrition numbers.
   C. Prepare materials with simple exercise principles attendees can use to implement a specific and individual exercise plan that is safe, effective, and efficient.
   D. Prepare deliverables attendees will be able to take with them after the workshop.

2. Implementation
   A. Work with you and your staff pre-workshop to answer questions and determine what is needed for final set up and preparation.
   B. We will provide a sample email for advertising the upcoming workshop throughout the company in order to

maximize attendance. We recommend an email blast 3 times per week for the 2 weeks prior to the workshop.

YOUR RESPONSIBILITIES

This project demands some involvement by your accounting personnel. Ultimate success is dependent on their effort. To help achieve a smooth and successful implementation, it will be your responsibility to:

1. Coordinate a date for the workshop to take place.
2. Coordinate an appropriate workshop area with ample room for all attendees.
3. Provide projector for Power point presentation and ensure attendees will be able to see and hear speaker.
4. Provide copies of handout materials and deliverables for all attendees.
5. Properly make it known throughout the company that the workshop is coming up and for employees to make time and save the date. We find a 2 week lead time sufficient and successful. Many times employees may not even know about valuable programs their company is supplying.
6. It will be up to the company to choose to add or provide some sort of incentive for attendance or not.

BENEFITS of Weight Management and Consistent Exercise Programs

Disease Prevention
Many diseases have been linked to poor diet and lack of exercise. Heart disease is the number one leading cause of

death in both men and women in the United States. Foods that you choose strongly influence the health of your heart; so better dietary habits can greatly reduce your risk for heart disease. Scientific evidence suggests that about 1/3 of cancer deaths that occur in the U.S. each year are due to nutrition and physical activity including obesity. For the majority of Americans who do not use tobacco, dietary choices and physical activity are the most important modifiable determinants of cancer risk.

Weight Control/Reduce Obesity
Research is still proving that there is no magic wand to wave to eliminate obesity. The best and safest way to lose and keep unwanted fat off the body is by eating a proper diet and consistent exercise.

Bone Loss Prevention
Calcium has always been the chosen key for building and maintaining strong bones, but the mineral cannot be absorbed without sufficient vitamin D levels. A healthy menu plan designed to prevent bone loss is so important especially for women experiencing or reaching menopause.

Lowers Cholesterol
Eating a heart healthy/low cholesterol diet can reduce your LDL blood cholesterol levels and ultimately reduce your risk for heart disease.

Teaches Healthier Eating Habits
A weight management program teaches you how to eat healthier and helps you develop lifelong habits of self-

control and mental stability. Eating smaller meals throughout the day to speed up your metabolism is just one example.

Increased Quality of Life

Gives you strength and stamina to be able to ride your bike, hike a mountain or go swimming with your children. We all want quality and without it, there is no quantity!

Increased Self Esteem and Productivity

Last but not least, it increases the way you feel about yourself and the world around you. Unfortunately, our self-esteem decreases with weight gain. Serious cases of weight gain can even lead to depression and medications. Imagine your food intake being the answer to your lifelong struggle of feeling really good about your life and accomplishing your goals.

COSTS AND PROFESSIONAL FEES

There are no professional fees that the company will incur for this workshop. It is purely an educational presentation that the company can feel free to make the most of and improve its' environment and company culture.

CLOSING

We appreciate the opportunity to present for your company. If you want to accept this proposal, please sign one copy and return it either in email or to the fax number below. Thank you!

Sincerely,

Chris Lutz
Master Trainer
S.P.A.R.T.A.
info@spartatraining.com
Fax: 206-XXX-XXXX

Having a Standard of Professionalism

One easy way to market yourself and stand out is to have a standard of professionalism. Many in the industry don't take it seriously or operate as if it is a real career or job. You've already taken a good step in buying and implementing the systems in this book. You'll want to look the part as well. You may not want to wear a shirt and tie at work unless you start more of a medical fitness or clinical exercise business. You'll want your attire to match the scope of what you'll be doing. We find that if you wear nice polo shirts, with your logo on it, of course, and khakis or slacks with some kind of comfortable dress shoe, you'll appear professional in what you are doing. You'll be doing some physical work setting equipment and spotting or assisting. A dress code much more formal than this is probably impractical and clients may find it odd or intimidating for the situation.

5 PROSPECTING FOR NEW CLIENTS

Market Development Inventory:

Next to each job or industry write down the names and numbers or email of anyone you even remotely know in this industry. This is to establish your network and sphere of influence. Work backwards from an annual revenue goal with the prospecting goal setting worksheet.

Use the scripts to call or email people you know (not cold call, but business associates, etc. you already know) in your network who might know someone who's a good candidate for what you do. Follow up scripts and lead qualification questions are also included.

Use the daily call reporting worksheet to keep track of your efforts.

We do this all the time especially through email or other social avenues like FB and Linked In with awesome results. Add this to your arsenal and teach it to your trainers and hopefully they'll have some good results over time. If they get their numbers right, over the course of a year, statistically, it will pan out to be pretty accurate.

A

Actor
Actuary
Advertising
Advocate
Aeronautical Engineer
Aerospace Industry Trades
Agricultural Economist
Agricultural Engineer
Agricultural Extension Officer
Agricultural Inspector
Agricultural Technician
Agriculture
Agriculturist
Agronomist
Air Traffic Controller
Ambulance Emergency Care Worker
Animal Scientist
Anthropologist
Aquatic Scientist
Archaeologist
Architect
Architectural Technologist
Archivist
Area Manager

Armament Fitter
Armature Winder
Art Editor
Artist
Assayer Sampler
Assembly Line Worker
Assistant Draughtsman
Astronomer
Attorney
Auctioneer
Auditor
Automotive Body Repairer
Automotive Electrician
Automotive Mechinist

Automotive Trimmer

B
Babysitting Career
Banking Career
Beer Brewing
Biochemist
Biokineticist
Biologist
Biomedical Engineer
BiomedicalTechnologist
Blacksmith
Boilermaker
Bookbinder
Bookkeeper
Botanist
Branch Manager
Bricklayer
Bus Driver
Business Analyst
Business Economist
Butler

C
Cabin Attendant
Carpenter
Cartographer
Cashier
Ceramics Technologist
Chartered Accountant
Chartered Management Accountant
Chartered Secretary
Chemical Engineer
Chemist
Chiropractor
City Treasurer
Civil Engineer
Civil Investigator
Cleaner

Clergyman
Clerk
Clinical Engineering
Clinical Technologist
Clothing Designer
Clothing Manager
Coal Technologist
Cobbler
Committee Clerk
Computer Industry
Concrete Technician
Conservation and Wildlife
Construction Manager
Copy Writer
Correctional Services
Costume Designer
Crane Operator
Credit Controller
Crop Protection and Animal Health
Customer and Excise Officer
Customer Service Agent

D
Dancer
Database Administrator
Data Capturer
Dealer in Oriental Carpets
Decor Designer
Dental Assistant and Oral Hygienist
Dental Technician
Dental Therapist
Dentist
Detective
Diamond Cutting
Diesel Fitter
Diesel loco Driver
Diesel Mechanic
Die-sinker and Engraver
Dietician

Diver
DJ
Domestic Appliance Mechanician
Domestic Personnel
Domestic radio and Television Mechanician
Domestic Worker
Draughtsman
Driver and Stacker

E
Earth Moving Equipment Mechanic
Ecologist
Economist Technician
Editor
Eeg Technician
Electrical and Electronic Engineer
Electrical Engineering Technician
Electrician
Electrician (Construction)
Engineering
Engineering Technician
Entomologist
Environmental Health Officer
Estate Agent
Explosive Expert
Explosive Technologist
Extractive Metallurgist

F
Farmer
Farm Foreman
Farm Worker
Fashion Buyer
Film and Production
Financial and Investment Manager
Fire-Fighter
Fireman at the Airport
Fitter and Turner
Flight Engineer

Florist
Food Scientist and Technologist
Footwear
Forester Service
Funeral Director
Furrier

G
Game Ranger
Gardener
Geneticist
Geographer
Geologist
Geotechnologist
Goldsmith and Jeweller
Grain Grader
Graphic Designer
Gravure machine Minder

H
Hairdresser
Herpetologist
Home Economist
Homoeopath
Horticulturist
Hospitality Industry
Hospital Porter
Human Resource Manager
Hydrologist

I
Ichthyologist
Industrial Designer
Industrial Engineer
Industrial Engineering Technologist
Industrial Technician
Inspector
Instrument Maker
Insurance

Interior Designer
Interpreter
Inventory and Store Manager
J
Jeweler
Jockey
Joiner and Woodmachinist
Journalist

K
Knitter

L
Labourer
Land Surveyor
Landscape Architect
Law
Learner Official
Leather Chemist
Leather Worker
Lecturer
Librarian
Life-guard
Lift Mechanic
Light Delivery Van Driver
Linesman
Locksmith

M
Machine Operator
Machine Worker
Magistrate
Mail Handler
Make-up Artist
Management Consultant
Manager
Marine Biologist
Marketing
Marketing Manager

Materials Engineer
Mathematician
Matron
Meat Cutting Technician
Mechanical Engineer
Medical Doctor
Medical Orthotist Prosthetist
Medical Physicist
Merchandise Planner
Messenger
Meteorological Technician
Meteorologist
Meter-reader
Microbiologist
Miner
Mine Surveyor
Mining Engineer
Model Builder
Model
Motor Mechanic
Musician

N
Nature Conservator
Navigating Officer
Navigator
Nuclear Scientist
Nursing
Nutritionist

O
Occupational Therapist
Oceanographer
Operations Researcher
Optical Dispenser
Optical Technician
Optometrist
Ornithologist

P
Painter and Decorator
Paint Technician
Paper Technologist
Patent Attorney
Personal Trainer
Personnel Consultant
Petroleum Technologist
Pharmacist Assistant
Pharmacist
Photographer
Physicist
Physiologist
Physiotherapist
Piano Tuner
Pilot
Plumber
Podiatrist
Police Officer
Post Office Clerk
Power Plant Operator
Private Secretary
Production Manager
Projectionist
Project Manager
Psychologist
Psychometrist
Public Relations Practitioner
Purchasing Manager

Q
Quality Control Inspector
Quantity Surveyor

R
Radiation Protectionist
Radio
Radiographer
Receptionist

Recreation Manager
Rigger
Road Construction Plant Operator
Roofer
Rubber Technologist

S
Salesperson
Sales Representative
Saw Operator
Scale Fitter
Sea Transport Worker
Secretary
Security Officer
Sheetmetal Worker
Shop Assistant
Shopfitter
Singer
Social Worker
Sociologist
Soil Scientist
Speech and Language Therapist
Sport Manager
Spray Painter
Statistician
Swimming Pool Superintendent
Systems Analyst

T
Tailor
Taxidermist
Teacher
Technical Illustrator
Technical Writer
Teller
Terminologist
Textile Designer
Theatre Technology
Tourism Manager

Traffic Officer
Translator
Travel Agent
Typist

V
Valuer and Appraiser
Vehicle Driver
Veterinary Nurse
Veterinary Surgeon
Viticulturist

W
Watchmaker
Weather Observer
Weaver
Welder
Wood Scientist
Wood Technologist

Y
Yard Official

Z
Zoologist

Prospecting Goal Setting

Work backwards from your annual income goal. Statistically, over a 12 month period, you should be on track to reach your goal.

Annual Income Goal: _____

Personal Income Per Deal: _____

Number of Deals Needed: _____

Monthly Deals Needed: _____

Consultations Needed/Deal	_____
Consultations Needed/Month	_____
Leads Needed/Consultation	_____
Leads Needed/Month	_____
Contacts Needed/Leads	_____
Contacts Needed/Month	_____
Days Worked/Month	_____
Contacts Needed/ Day	_____

S.P.A.R.T.A. Prospecting Script for Center of Influence

(You are calling people you know from your Market Development Inventory.)

Hi, this is _____. This is a business call, is this a good time to talk for a minute? Who do you know that could benefit from the type of training services we offer? Can you think of anyone in your (church group, family, neighborhood, or office), that may need my services at this time? XXXXX Great! Would you mind if I gave them a call or email? By the way, do you currently work with a trainer or go to a gym? XXXXX Terrific!

Client Just Signed Script (a day or two after sign up)

Hi Mrs. Jones, this is_____ from S.P.A.R.T.A. Personal Training, thank you again for coming in and signing up with us. I'm really excited about how you're going to do. While I'm thinking of it, most of the business we do it word of mouth. Do you know of anyone that would like to or could benefit from our program as you're about to? XXXXX Great! Would you mind if I gave them a call or email? Thank you very much!

Script for calling the prospect

Hi Mrs. Smith, my name is _____from S.P.A.R.T.A. Personal Training, this is a sales call about our new personal training program, is this a good time? You're friend, Mrs. Jones, just signed up with us to join our exercise program with goals of improving her body shape and increasing strength and stamina and mentioned your name as someone that might be interested in and could benefit from a program like this. Did you know we offer FREE consultations which includes a FREE workout with a certified trainer? Would you like to set one up? Which time is better for you Mon at XXXpm or Tues at XXXpm? Great! Thanks for taking the time to speak with me, I'll see you Mon at XXXpm.

Pre-Qualify 100% of Prospects. You can mix these questions in smoothly upon the prospects first call to you.

- How did you hear about me/us?
- What are you trying to achieve from working out?
- Are you planning to interview more than one trainer for the job?
- Are you working out on your own currently?
- Can you fit 2-3 workouts per weeks in your schedule?
- Is this 100% your decision or do you have to discuss this with somebody?
- If you feel this program is right for you can you afford ($?$?$?) per session/month? Or…
- My clients currently pay $60 per session, does that work for you?
- If after the workout you feel this is right for you, are you ready to start right away?

And, of course, keep track of your prospecting efforts to make sure that you are staying on track with your annual goal.

Daily Call Reporting

Summary of Daily Total Numbers (from above):

Monday: Thursday:

Contacts:_____   Contacts: _____

Consults:_____   Consults: _____

Contracts:_____   Contracts:_____

Tuesday: Friday:

Contacts: _____   Contacts: _____

Consults: _____   Consults: _____

Contracts:_____   Contracts:_____

Wednesday: Weekly Totals:

Contacts:_____   Contacts: _____

Consults:_____   Consults: _____

Contracts:_____   Contracts:_____

6 OPERATIONS

Client Intake Form Sample

Name:_____

Address:_____

City: _____ State: _____ Zip code:_____

Employer: _____

Job Title:_____

Day Telephone: _____

Eve Telephone: _____

Mobile Phone: _____

Email: _____

How did you hear about us?:_____

Notice: Email will be used for appointment notification purposes. We do not sell or distribute our client lists.

Gender: _____ Male _____ Female

Birth date: _____

Please check all that apply:

CONDITIONand EXPLAIN

Arthritis

Blood Clots

Cancer/Tumors

Chronic Pain (Explain Below)

Depression

Diabetes

Fatigue

Headaches

High/Low Blood Pressure

Muscle or Joint Pain (Explain Below)

Numbness/Tingling (Explain Below)

Other that may impact your ability to work out (Explain Below)

Scoliosis

Sinus Problems

Sleep Difficulties

Sprains/Strains (Explain Below)

Tendonitis (Explain Below)

Varicose Veins

Vision Problems

Explanation of any conditions listed above that require more detail:

Do you have a family history of any of the above conditions? Explain:

List any medications that you are currently taking that may have an effect on exercise:

List any allergies that you have:

List all previous major injuries/surgeries:

List any current/ongoing medical treatment that you are receiving:

List physical activities that you participate in regularly:

How many times per day do you usually eat?

List your primary activity at work? (i.e. On phone, sitting, computer, driving, etc.)

What do you do to relieve stress?

Have you participated in any kind of strength/circuit training before?

What obstacles/challenges have you encountered before in health and fitness?

What successes have you had?

On a scale of 1-10, how ready are you to make a change in your body?

Briefly describe why you feel you are a good candidate for a health and fitness investment with S.P.A.R.T.A.

What are your health and fitness goals for the next 12 months? Why did you contact us?

I understand the risks of fitness training should I not disclose pertinent health information. To my knowledge this information is complete and accurate and I will provide additional details should my condition change.

Signature_____ Date_____

Emergency Contact Person:

_____

Emergency phone: _____

Relationship to emergency contact: _____

Medical Contact Information (Required):

It is important that we communicate with other medical professionals responsible for your health. We may need to contact them to educate the proper professionals on the details of your program with S.P.A.R.T.A. This way, we can work closer together to fully obtain the best health and fitness possible for you. S.P.A.R.T.A.'s scope of practice does not involve the prescription of drugs, diagnosis or treatment of conditions or injuries, manipulation of skeletal structures, or application of therapeutic modalities. S.P.A.R.T.A. leaves those techniques to those respective specialists. Likewise, it is important that these professionals let S.P.A.R.T.A. know all of the pertinent client information so that a S.P.A.R.T.A. training™ specialist can properly prescribe the correct, safe, and custom exercise plan so that we can continue to work together on an ongoing basis.

This information is particularly important if you are a client that has special considerations such as hypertension, diabetes, or cardiovascular disease. It is also important if you have orthopedic injuries and/or are engaged in a post-rehab program with us. Please list the contact info for your primary doctor, orthopedist, physical therapist, chiropractor, or other relevant medical professionals:

Name: _____Type:_____
Phone/email:_____

Name: _____Type: _____
Phone/email:_____

Name: _____ Type: _____
Phone/email: _____

Liability Waiver:

I, the undersigned, being aware of my own health and physical condition, and having knowledge that my participation in any exercise program may be injurious to my health, am voluntarily participating in physical activity with S.P.A.R.T.A.

Having such knowledge, I hereby release S.P.A.R.T.A., their representatives, agents, and successors from liability for accidental injury or illness which I may incur as a result of participating in the said physical activity. I hereby assume all risks connected therewith and consent to participate in said program.

I agree to disclose any physical limitations, disabilities, ailments, or impairments which may affect my ability to participate in said fitness program.

Signature: _____ Date: _____

Cancellation/Reschedule Policy for Sessions:

All cancellations must be received at least 12 hours before your training session in order to avoid being charged for your session. Clients who do not cancel with 12 hours notice will be charged for the cancelled session. S.P.A.R.T.A. understands that emergencies happen. We provide every client with one free short-notice cancellation. You will not be charged for your first cancellation with less than 12 hour notice. The free short-notice cancellation only applies if S.P.A.R.T.A. is notified prior to the session start time. No shows are not eligible for the free cancellation. You may reschedule your appointments for other times as make ups.

If you need to cancel a session altogether without make up, please contact your trainer as soon as possible.

Refund Policy:

NO RISK! S.P.A.R.T.A. strives to provide the best possible service to our clients. If for any reason you are not satisfied with our services after 30 days, we will be happy to issue you a refund. If you have paid for a package in full, you will be refunded for unused sessions and services.

I have read the above policies and agree to its terms as it applies to my personal training.

Signature: _____ Date: _____

FREE TRIAL WORKOUT at this point

Training with S.P.A.R.T.A.

Your health and fitness investment with S.P.A.R.T.A. includes:

FREE month of training.
FREE fitness assessments (body fat%, circumference measurements, etc.).
FREE 3 step fat loss guide upon sign up.
Guaranteed results!!!

Good: 2 times per week plan with ($65/session)

Better: 3 times per week plan with ($60/session)

Best Value: 4 times per week plan ($55/session)

Each plan has a 1 time initiation/startup fee $150 A low monthly gym membership fee will be charged to your card starting NEXT month.

Plans are based only on a month to month commitment and are calculated on an eight (8) session (2 times per week), twelve (12) session (3 times per week), or sixteen (16) session (4 times per week) basis. This means that over the course of a year, you are actually getting a FREE month (8 or 12 or 16 sessions) in that years' time. Session make ups are available. Plans are paid monthly and you'll be automatically renewed each month for as long as you wish.

Referral Program

Most of our new business is word of mouth referrals. We want you to look and feel great and continue to bring us new business. In return, we will reward your efforts by giving you a FREE MONTH for every 4 people who sign up that you refer!

Credit Card Authorization Form

I, _____, hereby grant permission to S.P.A.R.T.A. to automatically charge my credit card for $ _____ for personal fitness training on the

    1st   or   15th (circle one) of the month.

☐ I also authorize S.P.A.R.T.A. to maintain this credit card information on file to pay for monthly services rendered.

    Credit Card #:_____
    Expiration: _____
    CV2 Code: _____ (3 digits on back)

Name on Card: _____

Billing Address on

Card:_____

_____

Telephone on Card: _____

Signature: _____ Date: _____

If you'll be working in your own studio or health club, you'll need to lease or buy space. There are a lot of mistakes that can be made in this process. What if it is on the second floor? Can you even get your heavy equipment up there? Those kinds of things will have to be taken into consideration as well as more legal and political considerations having to do with operating a business in your local area. Use the worksheet below to properly identify all the factors that will be relevant to your business operating in your area.

Office Lease Check list

Property:_____ Date Viewed:_____
Rent:_____ Sq. Ft:_____ ___
Lease Term:_____ When Available:_____
Payment Due Date:_____ Contract Available:_____
Deposit:_____ Parking Availability:____
Security in Place:_____ Structural Insurance:____

Utilities: Use of:
 - Water/Power/AC: - Conference Room:
 - Phone: - Bathroom/change:
 - Internet: - Kitchen:

Access by Employees after hours/weekends:

Lease Restrictions/Zoning:

Floor wt. restrictions:

Early Termination of Lease by Tenant:

Early Termination of Lease by Landlord:

Option to Renew:

Modifications to Office:

Remedy for Service Interruption:

Responsibility for Repairs:

Conditions for Return of Property:

Specifications for Signs:

Layout Notes:

Realize that NOT operating out of your own brick and mortar facility can keep your costs and responsibilities down, but there are tradeoffs. If you operate out of client homes or work places, you will likely spend a significant amount of time driving between them in your area. Time is money! You'll need to charge accordingly to make up for that lost time or find another unique way around making up that difference where you can't see clients while you are in the car.

Perhaps, if you have the money, the best compromise might be to rent space or contract in an established health club. Early on, without a lot of capital, your best agreement here will likely be a percentage of each session you perform. But, again, be prepared to give up as much as 40% to the business owner you'll be renting from. If you have more of a clientele established, a flat rent fee may suit you better. This will be something you'll have to research and negotiate with the available facilities in your area.

The good news is, there are ways you can maximize your time should you choose to operate in a mobile fashion.

How to Double Your Income as a Personal Trainer Blueprint
Or Give Yourself More Free Time Without Sacrificing Your Personal Training Revenue

Just a couple of years ago, no personal trainer or personal training association would have ever thought to have suggested that clients workout for shorter amounts of time. But, that's exactly the case I'm going to make here. The best part is that it won't skimp on anything and might even increase client results. It will certainly double the time that you have available to take on paying clients or give yourself more free time.

Classically, the typical personal training session lasts 1 hour. I'm here to tell you that you can convert all of your 1 hour clients into half hour sessions so that you can now see 2 people in an hour and double your income. I have been instructing 1 on 1 personal training workouts for over 10 years and have NEVER performed an hour long session. There are numerous ways that you can perform a quality 1 on 1 session in half the time. It just so happens that we use an approach which has always been a duration of around 30 minutes. Basically, we perform full body, single set programs, to voluntary muscular fatigue on each exercise, and move QUICKLY between each exercise to maximize cardiovascular involvement too. You're addressing 2 components of a client's fitness program here.

However, that's not the only way you can do it. The problem is that there is so much wasted time in a normal hour long workout. My good friend, Dr. Paul Kennedy, told a story one time where he timed a workout he saw a trainer doing in the gym with 2 stopwatches. 1 to record the total workout time and the other to record only when a set was being done. At the end, the total time was 57minutes and the total exercise time was about 3 minutes. That's because there's only a few seconds of super-fast reps for any given set followed by 3-5 minutes or more of rest or talking.

Let's do the math. If you did 10 sets, with only 3 minutes rest in between, that's 30 minutes of non-working time right there. If you rest 5 minutes and talk, walk around, get a drink, etc., that's already 50 minutes wasted. An effective and efficient workout is continuous activity for nearly the entire 30 minutes with a high heart rate. There might be 5 minutes left over to talk about calorie control or do a head to toe stretching routine with 20 second stretches for each area.

About 97% of the research shows that you can perform a quality set to voluntary muscular fatigue and that is just as effective as multiple sets. If you have been doing 3 set programs, you can eliminate 2/3 of the work without compromising effectiveness. That's absolutely true and I've been doing it for over a decade. You can attend to more than one component of your client's fitness in one program. Who doesn't like to kill 2 or 3 birds with one stone, right? If you still prefer to use multiple sets, you can use advanced techniques like breakdowns, some sort of superset arrangement, etc. Or just cut out some of the talking and move on. Clients also don't need you to babysit them and stand next to them on a treadmill if you choose to prescribe additional cardio. A simple direction and you're off to something else that is bringing you revenue. You could also have them come in 15 minutes early to do cardio and continue for an additional 15 minutes after resistance training with you. But, they will only pay for the 30 minutes they are with you. I'm not saying they will pay you less, on the contrary, you will actually be giving them more work and maybe more productive work in less time. Prospective clients will associate time with value. That's a mistake on their part and it's your job to educate them that it is far less about quantity and more about quality.

If they don't get equal or better results in less time and commitment for them, you can go back to hour long sessions. Of course, it will be just as effective assuming the exercise intensity is appropriate.

Get out of the mindset that you are trading your time for dollars. To an extent, you are, but in this case, you charge PER

SESSION. The session will be equally effective if not better because there is more work in shorter time. What do we call that? Intensity. Every trainer knows recent research is showing shorter duration, higher intensity workouts can be more metabolically effective and slash exercise time. Why waste a client's time? They can get back to work sooner and be more productive to make more money, themselves. Everyone is benefitting from this arrangement.

If you can offer half hour sessions and not glue yourself to the side of a treadmill while they walk on it, you just DOUBLED YOUR CAPACITY. You can now take on twice as many clients at the same PER SESSION rate as what other trainers are doing. Remember, you charge per session, not per hour. Your clients pay for results, not wasted time and your time and their's is valuable. If you're accustomed to making an average market price of $60/hour in exchange for your services, just imagine doubling that. You now make (AND ARE WORTH) $120/hour. Why would you leave half of your income on the table by not doing this?

Now, take it a step further. Most people don't have a lot of cash lying around in a down economy so lower cost small group training is an option. You can still get $60 or more in 30 minutes, but get $35 from 2 people that you see at the same time. It's a little less personal attention, but it's about half the cost for them and a little more for you. We call it semi-private training. It's good for couples or stay at home moms who are friends. The buddy system. A better bet would be to find a group of 3. Let's say you know 3 stay at home moms that would like to workout together. You can charge each $25 for a total of $75 in a half hour. Let's say you are really good and you get 2 small groups of 3 back to back and now you just made $150 in one hour. Does charging $60 per hour still seem like something you should be doing? Nearly everybody wants more money. Why not save your clients money and time and earn more (a LOT MORE) yourself in the process?

If you do a FREE hour long consultation with a client when they first come in, make sure to inform them in your marketing copy and in person that what they are getting is at least a $120 value for FREE. Start this immediately with all of your new prospects that come in and you'll be 2 steps ahead of all the other trainers in your area.

Incident Report Form

Date of Incident: _____

Date of Reporting: _____ (If not the same date, please provide written explanation for the delay in reporting the incident).

Name of Client: _____

Location of Incident: _____

Details of Incident:

_____
_____
_____
_____
_____
_____
_____
_____

Did client require medical treatment? _____

Was an ambulance called for treatment? _____

Who was present at time of incident?

_____

_____

Other information that pertains to the incident:

_____

Please fax incident forms to 703-XXX-XXXX or scan/email to info@spartatraining.com. In addition, please call Chris Lutz at 703-XXX-XXXX immediately to inform him of the incident.

Personal Training Medical Crisis Plan

Procedures:

All paper work must be filled out. Client Intake Forms (Medical history forms, emergency contact information forms, liability waiver, etc.) must be filled out prior to client's first session.

Trainer must be up to date on all 1st Aid, CPR, & AED training, and have a 1st Aid kit on site. The kit should be properly maintained and replenished as needed. Should a situation arise where the client is in need of minor first aid (scrape, bruise, etc...), the trainer will attend to the client, using 1st Aid materials that are available. Personal trainer cannot be held responsible for allergic reactions if not made aware prior to application. Should an emergency situation arise, the trainer will check the scene and make sure it is safe, and then check the victim.

The trainer will apply aid to the victim without moving them, unless they are in immediate danger. The trainer may instruct another person to call EMS. (If available) Otherwise the trainer will apply 2 minutes of aid and then call EMS. If the trainer has started CPR or aid with an AED, the trainer is NOT TO STOP once started and must direct someone else to call for help. Once EMS arrives, the trainer is responsible for providing them with the client's medical history as well as any other important information related to the incident as requested by EMS. No trainer shall act outside of their scope of practice or training they are up to date on.

Next the trainer will notify the emergency contact person supplied in the emergency contact information forms.

Miscellaneous:

During any type of natural disaster (tornado, hurricane, flood, etc.) shelter will be sought out in an area deemed safest given the current location. Any type of improper touch or verbal advances will be grounds for immediate termination of the session, and a refund will not be given. If the client is intoxicated during the session, the session will be canceled immediately, without refund. The trainer will keep a daily log of each session. The client's confidentiality will not be breached, and any use of client information for the purpose of advertising must be in the written form of consent. In the event one of the above situations should occur (or a situation or event similar), an incident report will be filled out.

7 YOUR REAL ESTATE ON THE WEB

If you can afford to work with a reputable and reliable web developer, go ahead and do it. Probably your best bet for being visible on the web is setting yourself up a Wordpress blog. www.wordpress.com. It serves as your website and a content management system that you can easily update and manage yourself on a regular basis.

Regular posts on your blog will help the search engines bring your site up higher in results with the more recent and relevant content that you add. Additionally, there are many plug-ins and different themes to use to customize it. More than one income stream can be created by creating membership areas or selling other products through your site. You can even hide things behind a password protected page or post on your site. If you use some of the resources listed earlier like Paypal and Google Checkout, you can easily place the code for payment buttons on your site to take payments not only from your local customers, but from potential customers all over the world. We'll go more into other income streams later.

But, understand this. Starting a personal training business is, most of the time, focusing on the local market. With tools like the internet, now you have the opportunity to scale up your business in numerous other ways, to disseminate your knowledge beyond your local community, and potentially become an international presence.

This chapter could go on forever, but I want to stop there and maybe leave the subject for the topic of another book. It's best to be simple at first and expand from there. A $10,000 website won't do you any good if you don't have any or it's not getting you any clients. There is absolutely nothing wrong with investing in professional looking graphics and a website. But, be careful and tread lightly here. Many people I know have been burned by the unprofessional the web development/design arena. The good thing about a Wordpress site is it can be very basic and you can ramp it up to infinite complexity from there without the need to change much or redo an entire site.

At the very least, you'll want your site to market you or your business with who you are, what you do, where you're located, and why potential clients should choose you. Make sure you include a call to action for them to DO something before they leave your page. Either opt-in to your email list through your web form (that you get through Aweber) which sits on your home page. Or that they should call you to set up a free consultation/workout. Attach some kind of time sensitive promotion to initiate action from them.

8 FINANCIALS

Earlier I mentioned that we got started and off the ground with the revenue from the first client or two. This will depend on what type of model you'll want to implement. Ideally, you'll have only or mostly variable costs meaning that you'll only have costs if you make something first. That is doable for the most part. However, if you're going to start a studio or larger gym, you'll have much more in the way of up front capital (equipment) and fixed costs (rent, etc.). You can secure funding for ventures like this from loans from your bank or credit union. However, in a tight lending economy it might be tough to secure. You can also find an investor or more than one to put together what you need. You'll need a complete and well thought out business plan to present to them in order to have confidence in your ability to make it profitable and pay them back. Friends and family can be an early source of startup funding, but beware, this can strain personal relationships. It's always the initial building process that is the hardest to get over until you reach that "critical mass" so to speak. You want to be able to show that you reasonably believe you can get the venture off the ground using their money and be able to pay them back plus whatever interest or equity is agreed upon.

Pricing your service. A quick and informal way to do some local market research is to do a Google search for "personal trainer XYZ town". Go through and try to find all the training company's sites that list their rates. You can get a good idea of what everyone is charging. We'll call that the market price. You can charge right in that range and expect a reasonable amount of customers. You can charge just below that and compete on price. We wouldn't recommend that, but it is a strategy. Or, there is such a thing known as perceived value. The idea here is that if it is the most expensive thing out there, it must be the best. Or at least that's what some consumers might think. But, consumers, although they may not appear rational sometimes, are a lot smarter than that. I'd advise if you were to take this approach, you had better be ready to back it up really well. More than likely, you'll fall close to market price, but the challenge for you is to differentiate well enough to where competing on price is not even on the consumer's radar. Once you get an idea of what you'd like to charge, use the example above in our client consultation forms for how to frame your pricing to present it to potential clients when they come in for a consultation.

Equipment concerns. This is a big concern. A lot of money can be spent on making a facility look nice and shiny, but in reality be filled with junk equipment. I would not go directly to equipment makers for a line of their best stuff. I've purchased enough equipment to fill about 2 studios worth for very little. Check what equipment is available that is used. You can clean up and piece together a very nice looking set up of free weights for not too much capital. You'll want Olympic bars and weight plates. That is the standard for free weight training. For smaller exercises or women, you might want to have on hand a Standard bar and plate set. Standard bars have the smaller 1 inch diameter holes in the plates. You'll want at least an adjustable bench and a power rack. Always, always, always use a rack with self-spotting bars in place if you have it. The power rack is an extremely versatile piece you can perform a vast array of exercises in and it is infinitely safer too if you use it correctly. As long as you use and set the safety bars/stops, there will be no accidents. Your main challenges then become moving, shipping, or storing this equipment. Shipping items like these are very expensive, because of the weight involved.

Honestly, for machinery, should you choose to use it, I'd recommend looking for the used Nautilus equipment that is out there. It's biomechanically correct and it lasts forever. There are still companies that will re-upholster padding and make hand grips and the like in case those superficial parts wear out. You might even consider the plate loaded machinery. Although the steel frames are still heavy, they are sometimes easier to transport than the selectorized machines with the weight stack attached. Plate loaded machines use Olympic plates which will match your free weight set so all of the resistance is universal. Plate loaded machines are attractive to men to train on, but will present some efficiency problems for you as the trainer. You have to continuously load and unload hundreds of pounds all day long. That can get very tiring and present an opportunity for injury too. Some plate loaded exercises are not quite as biomechanically correct as their selectorized counterparts. Nothing is perfect, this is where you will have to make some decisions based on these tradeoffs as to what is best for you and your business. I have about a 300 square foot home studio containing everything I listed above that I put together for approximately $1500. All of the colors match too. Some of the equipment is pushing 40 years old, but still works just like the day it came out of the factory. I've only painted superficially and tightened up inner workings like chains and belts. Other than that, besides regular cleaning of pads, it requires little in the way of maintenance attention and is 100% reliable.

If you'll be starting out or your model is to travel to client homes or workplaces, you'll need lighter equipment that you can transport easily. You'll also likely need to brush up on your technical skills for manual resistance which can be a very effective form of training for little equipment involved. Again, the tradeoff here is that it can be costly travel time to you and tiring over the course of a day as you'll likely be close to as much work as the client is.

You can do virtually any equipment exercise, with some exceptions, in a manual fashion. There are some rules to follow. Be sure each partner understands. It is the trainee's responsibility to maintain control and change directions before reaching a point of over stretching as in neck exercises. Also, the trainee should not off/on their effort or suddenly give out on any exercise as the partner will still steadily be applying force. The partner must start slow gradually increasing force application with each rep until there is enough that the trainee will fatigue in the prescribed rep range. You may want to progressively work up to full range especially in the stretched position. For example, only go half way down on the first rep, slightly farther on the next, and then finally, a full but comfortable stretch on the 3rd or 4th rep. Be absolutely certain the client knows not to relax in the stretched position, but to maintain tension and perform a smooth and fluid change of direction into the next positive. Repeatedly mention this. It will be very tempting for them to let off suddenly while you are applying a fair amount of force. Remember also, that you need to vary the resistance. You should apply more force where they are stronger and slightly let off to allow them to complete the positive where they are weaker mechanically. To add an extra layer of difficulty, once you have developed a good bit of fatigue in the trainee, the partner can gradually decrease force application for an additional few reps. I've done this with the manual tricep extension until someone cannot even lift the weight of their forearm up and I'm barely touching their hand to apply resistance.

Make no mistake about this; manual training is a skill that is acquired with lots and lots of practice. Each client is a new experience and each one you will have to instruct and work with differently. Remember that wherever you are applying force to a client's body, you probably have a massive leverage advantage over them. You may not realize it, but just a slight push from you can place a HUGE amount of force on their tissues at the other end of their bony levers. This can especially be true in the neck. Sometimes, it may be just appropriate to start with the weight of the client's own limb or maybe just the weight of your hands. **Be extra, extra careful. I cannot emphasize this enough.** There have been many instances of Yoga instructors pushing on clients in stretched positions and snapping their tendons off the bones. Not just Yoga, but anyone who doesn't fully appreciate the forces that you can impart from your hands through a client's limbs and onto their soft tissues. It may not be for everyone and it may be the only thing some can tolerate as a substitute for other movements. Use your judgment on each client and act prudently.

Keep in mind that expenses like office supplies, your computers, your cell phone, and even your car can be owned by the business or paid for through it. Many of these things can be positive for you on your taxes. Ask for a checklist from your accountant of what to keep track of during the year so that you can possibly write off when tax time comes. Always set aside extra money to pay your taxes. As I said earlier, paying estimated quarterly taxes will probably be easiest for you. You are now the employer, no one will be withholding taxes automatically for you out of your paycheck any more. You'll have to anticipate what you're likely to make and set that aside in order to pay each quarter. A lot can happen in 3 months so beware of that and try your best to plan accordingly especially if you tend to have slow times during the year.

9 STAFFING

In prior chapters I mentioned getting out of the mindset of charging per hour and gave some ways to get around that scenario. Regardless, there is an upper limit to what we can do ourselves. In which case, when it comes time, you may want to try to scale your business up further by replicating yourself or hiring more trainers to work with you. This can also free you up to hopefully move out of your daily training responsibilities and focus more on growing more of the revenue generating parts of your business. This is known as working ON your business rather than working IN your business. It's a real challenge for all entrepreneurs, but you'll want to start to think that way if you ever want your business to grow to something beyond just you or if you'd like to sell it one day.

Below, we will give you some of the tools you'll need to get started bringing potential new hires as trainers.

Employee/Independent Contractor Application

APPLICANT INFORMATION			
Last Name	First	M.I.	Date
Street Address		Apartment/Unit #	
City	State		ZIP
Phone		E-mail Address	
Date Available	Social Security No.		Desired Salary

Position Applied for				
Are you a citizen of the United States?	YES ☐	NO ☐	If no, are you authorized to work in the U.S.?	YES ☐ NO ☐
Have you ever worked for this company?	YES ☐	NO ☐	If so, when?	
Have you ever been convicted of a felony?	YES ☐	NO ☐	If yes, explain	

EDUCATION

High School		Address		
From	To	Did you graduate? YES ☐ NO ☐		Degree
College		Address		
From	To	Did you graduate? YES ☐ NO ☐		Degree
Other		Address		
From	To	Did you graduate? YES ☐ NO ☐		Degree

REFERENCES

Please list three professional references.

Full Name	Relationship	
Company	Phone	( )
Address		
Full Name	Relationship	
Company	Phone	( )
Address		
Full Name	Relationship	
Company	Phone	( )
Address		

PREVIOUS EMPLOYMENT

Company		Phone ( )	
Address		Supervisor	
Job Title	Starting Salary $	Ending Salary $	
Responsibilities			
From To	Reason for Leaving		

Lutz

May we contact your previous supervisor for a reference?	YES ☐ NO ☐		
Company		Phone ( )	
Address		Supervisor	
Job Title	Starting Salary $	Ending Salary $	
Responsibilities			
From To	Reason for Leaving		

May we contact your previous supervisor for a reference?	YES ☐ NO ☐		
Company		Phone ( )	
Address		Supervisor	
Job Title	Starting Salary $	Ending Salary $	
Responsibilities			
From To	Reason for Leaving		

May we contact your previous supervisor for a reference?	YES ☐ NO ☐

MILITARY SERVICE			
Branch		From To	
Rank at Discharge		Type of Discharge	
If other than honorable, explain			

Applicant Questions (Attach additional pages if necessary.)

Why should we hire you?

_____
_____
_____
_____

What skills do you already have? What skills do you hope to develop?

_____
_____
_____
_____

What type of job do you see yourself perusing next? When? Where?

_____
_____
_____
_____

What can you tell us about you personally? (Hobbies, interests, acknowledgements, etc.)

_____
_____
_____
_____

Do you have any questions?

_____
_____
_____
_____
_____
_____

DISCLAIMER AND SIGNATURE

I certify that my answers are true and complete to the best of my knowledge.

If this application leads to employment, I understand that false or misleading information in my application or interview
may result in my release.

Signature   Date

Offer Letter

Dear XXX,

S.P.A.R.T.A. is pleased to offer you the position of high intensity training specialist. In this position you will be reporting to either Indra Books in administration or Chris Lutz, owner. The starting salary offered for this position is commission based at $18.75 for each half hour session performed. In the case of a small group of 2 people, $20/half hour, or 3 people, 26.25/half hour. There are other compensation methods especially for in home training and other general duties as assigned. Pay periods are every two weeks. Your start date with S.P.A.R.T.A. can be immediate and you will be working from primarily Fairfax and Loudoun county locations. This offer will expire 12 midnight on 3/31/10.

Please note that your employment with the company is for no specified period and constitutes "at will" employment. As a result, you are free to resign at any time, for any reason or for no reason. Similarly, the company is free to terminate its employment relationship with you at any time, with or without cause.

Your acceptance of this offer and commencement of employment with the company are contingent upon your execution of the company's standards and philosophy.

On your first day of employment, you will be provided with additional information about the objectives and policies, benefit programs and general employment conditions. To fulfill federal identification requirements, you should bring documentation to support your identity (I-9 form) and eligibility to work in the United States.

We are pleased to have you join the S.P.A.R.T.A.'s team as a member of what we feel is an organization that offers each employee an opportunity for personal and professional development. If you have any questions, please do not hesitate to contact me at 703-XXX-XXXX. We look forward to working with you in the future, and hope you will find your employment at S.P.A.R.T.A. a rewarding experience.

S.P.A.R.T.A.

ACCEPTED AND AGREED:

_____   Date: _____
              Signature

_____
              Name

_____
              Title

By:_____   Date:_____
         Candidate Signature

_____
              Name

Employee/Independent Contractor Agreement

Independent Contractor Status

As an Independent Contractor, you commit to S.P.A.R.T.A. while being paid for a task. This means complete dedication to the job at that time. Our clients expect nothing less than top notch service. While family needs are important to us, the client has to come first with this business. We cannot allow children or other adults not subject to this agreement to accompany ICs on tasks for any reason at any time.

S.P.A.R.T.A. will not maintain direct supervision or control over the acts of the Independent Contractor taken in furtherance of the contracted services. Therefore, the Independent Contractor at all times retains the absolute right to control and perform the contracted services by his/her own method and manner. The Independent Contractor is responsible for transportation to and from the assignment and is not acting in the course of the assignment during such transportation. The Independent Contractor will only receive payment for any purchases made for the client and/or any other flat fee agreed upon by both parties pursuant to the contracted engagement, and will not be reimbursed for any additional and extraneous expenses (e.g. transportation and time spent).

The Independent Contractor is in no respect an agent, employee, or legal representative of S.P.A.R.T.A. and shall have no power to bind S.P.A.R.T.A. or to assume or create any obligations on behalf or in the name of S.P.A.R.T.A.. S.P.A.R.T.A. will not treat the Independent Contractor as an employee for any purpose, including but not limited to, the Federal Insurance Contributions Act, the Social Security Act, the Federal Unemployment Act, income tax, workers' compensation, unemployment, insurance, or pension or profit sharing plans. The Independent Contractor shall be solely responsible for, and pay, all self-employment, income, and other taxes due on account of the Independent Contractor's relationship with S.P.A.R.T.A..

Fees:
The Independent Contractor will be paid by the task. The rate will be $ _____ for the duration of each task and the Independent Contractor must submit a time sheet in our client tracking database. Any time not entered within the given pay period will not be paid. Independent Contractors will be paid by pay cycles that run bi-weekly.

Releases:
The Independent Contractor hereby releases S.P.A.R.T.A. from and against all claims, suits, and actions based upon any personal

injury, illness, death, property damage, or any other loss sustained
by the Independent Contractor as a direct or indirect result of the
connection with his/her contracted services rendered to
S.P.A.R.T.A., such connection shall include but not be limited to
the following: transportation to and from the assignment, and
negligent or intentional acts or omissions attributable to the
assigned business. The Independent Contractor shall defend,
indemnify, and hold S.P.A.R.T.A. harmless from and against all
claims, suits, actions, general and special damages, costs
(including attorney fees), and expenses, including but not limited
to any personal injury, death, or property damage, resulting in
whole or in part from the breach by the Independent Contractor of
any of his/her obligations hereunder or from any negligent or
intentional act or omission attributable to the Independent
Contractor or any of his/her agents, assistants, or employees.

Retained Confidences/Non-compete
The Independent Contractor shall hold confidential all information
pertaining to S.P.A.R.T.A.'s client(s) obtained by the Independent
Contractor through his/her work with S.P.A.R.T.A.. The
Independent Contractor shall not communicate any such
information to any other person, company, or entity other than
S.P.A.R.T.A..

Furthermore, the Independent Contractor may not use information
gained from assignments or clients for S.P.A.R.T.A. to further
his/her own career in the field of personal training for a term of
one year after terminating the relationship with S.P.A.R.T.A.. For
a period of one year after separation, the Independent Contractor
will not, directly or indirectly solicit business of any client of
S.P.A.R.T.A. or any prospective client with whom S.P.A.R.T.A. is
in negotiations at the time of the separation.

The Independent Contractor agrees that at no time during or after
his tenure with S.P.A.R.T.A. shall he/she, directly or indirectly,
reveal, copy, divulge, transfer, or use for the benefit of any person
or entity other than S.P.A.R.T.A. any of S.P.A.R.T.A.'s confidential
or trade secret information. "Confidential or trade secret
information" as used in this clause shall mean information of

S.P.A.R.T.A.'s which is not generally known outside of S.P.A.R.T.A. and shall include, but not be limited to, confidential business processes, designs, formula, privileged legal information, software, pricing, and customer identities.

Term
The Independent Contractor agrees that the terms and restrictions of this agreement shall remain in effect for the duration of any assignment from the date of this agreement and shall apply to and be effective throughout the duration of any and all future assignments for S.P.A.R.T.A. without the necessity of re-signing this acknowledgment form.

Governing Law
The Independent Contractor agrees that the terms of this agreement will be governed by the laws of the Commonwealth of Virginia and agrees that the exclusive forum for any litigation hereunder shall be the courts of Virginia, federal or state as appropriate.

Please initial each paragraph after reading and complete the section below:

Printed Name:

Signature:

Date:

Employee Evaluation

1. What goals did you accomplish since your last evaluation (or hire)?
2. What goals were you unable to accomplish and what hindered you from achieving them?
3. What goals will you set for the next period?
4. What resources do you need from the organization to achieve these goals?

5. Based on YOUR personal satisfaction with your job (workload, environment, pay, challenge, etc.) how would you rate your satisfaction from 1 (poor) to 10 (excellent.)
1 2 3 4 5 6 7 8 9 10

*You do have to stress that question #5 is not how well they think they're doing their job, but how satisfied they are with the job.

This is a simple, but very effective review process you can do with staff members 90 days after hire and every 6 months thereafter. It's the simplicity that is the beauty. It won't take all day to do and you'll likely get truthful and accurate feedback from the employee.

Exit Interview

Name: Date:

	Strongly Agree	Agree	Neutral	Disagree	Strongly Disagree	N/A
Overall this job met my expectations and provided me with information I can use.	☐	☐	☐	☐	☐	☐
The projects were interesting and relevant to my career objectives.	☐	☐	☐	☐	☐	☐
The S.P.A.R.T.A. representative devoted enough time to me, my questions, and the experience in general.	☐	☐	☐	☐	☐	☐
Overall I would recommend this job to another person.	☐	☐	☐	☐	☐	☐

Which aspect did you enjoy the most? Why?

_____

_____

Which aspect did you enjoy the least? Why?

_____

Was the workload too much, too little, or just about right?

_____

Based on your experience with us, what do you think it takes to
succeed at this company?

_____

How do you generally feel about this company?

_____

What can we do to improve this experience for future employees?

_____

_____

Is there anything else about your experience here that you'd like to
share?

May we contact you in the future for follow-up, regarding leads, or for job opportunities within or outside S.P.A.R.T.A.?	☐ Yes ☐ No

10 MULTIPLE STREAMS OF INCOME

Rarely does an established business succeed in the long term with 1 product and 1 product only. It's all about staying agile and adaptable to the marketplace and consumer demands. You'll certainly have your core service offered and your specialties, but you'll also want to try to incorporate other income streams as you get up and running.

You might think, "What other options for income do personal trainers have?" As it turns out, our field is quite flexible and we can end up offering quite a bit. Here are some other examples of additional income streams offered by personal trainers.

- Small group/semi-private training
- Workshops/seminars/webinars
- Public speaking for a fee
- Offer online training
- Phone/email consultations
- Nutritional counseling
- Metabolic testing
- Supplement sales
- DVD sales
- Book or eBook sales
- Apparel
- Manuals
- Special certifications/ continuing education
- Consulting with other businesses
- Mentoring

- Software of some kind
- Equipment sales
- Membership to your website
- Joint venture/co-promotion/affiliate sales
- Special events
- Sponsorships
- Advertising in your facility or on your website

We've done all of the above in one fashion or another (you're reading one right now). There are almost limitless options. Your imagination is the only real limit. You don't need or want to ask permission to do these things. Just pick what you like or are strongest and go do it.

We've already talked about the model to do semi-private training. Once you get your skills down training clients 1 on 1, adding another client or 2 can be easy and profitable for you.

Above, you saw the proposal for a corporate wellness workshop. In order to build your credibility and reputation, you may need to engage in these things for free at first, but then when you are good at them and you are in demand, you can start charging for them. A corporate wellness or fitness workshop or some similar type of seminar is a great way to come across as an expert and make a nice revenue stream too. You can even do these kinds of things virtually through a webinar software. Anymeeting www.anymeeting.com is one of my favorites.

There are always organizations looking for speakers and fitness, fat loss, and health are topics that are always in demand and always will be for the foreseeable future. You can have organizations pay to have you travel to them or their conferences in various locations to give a speech on a certain topic relevant to them. You can probably track down opportunities like this through your current network.

Online training is another option to help more people and get your knowledge to go a lot farther than just your local market. You can do it as simply as phone/email coaching or you can use some of the online training software systems that are out there. These aren't perfect by any means, but may offer another way to connect with customers who otherwise you would not have been able to serve. eFitnesstracker www.efitnesstracker.com is one that we like. The admin set up is a little user unfriendly, but otherwise, it's a good service and they are excellent about keeping in touch and supporting you. Probably the hardest thing about online training is making the sale strictly over the internet without the face to face contact you'd have in person. But, this can be a great revenue stream to add to your business.

Here's a good rule of thumb I like to use in charging for online training. Take what you would charge for 1 session in person training and that is your monthly charge for online training. So, let's say you charge $70 for a single 1 on 1 training session in person, you'll charge $70/month for online. Now, $70/month isn't a whole lot of money so you'll have to make sure that your time investment into managing it isn't exceeding what it is worth. You want to deliver good quality programs online, but not take more time than you would to do it in person. This will be determined by how you set up the routines as well as the kind of software you choose. I would only prescribe workouts 1 week in advance. I'd send out the routines on Sunday and have the clients work through 3 full body routines throughout the week according to our principles we gave them. Then they would update each workout with what they were able to do and any feedback they had. I'd review again on Sunday and send out all of the progressions, substitutions, changes, new routines, then. So, I was really only working on it on a weekly basis 1 day a week. That was easy to manage for me and not too much of a time investment. Later on, I had our trainers manage their clients online too. I even had a trainer in Michigan (we work in Virginia) work virtually with clients online all over the country.

Along the same lines as doing a webinar, you can do phone and email consultations too. I do free 30 minute phone consultations with trainers first and then I charge $100/hour for phone consultations after that. You can use your business phone, landline, your cell phone or even Skype. www.skype.com. Skype even offers you the chance to use the video feature through your computer's web cam so that you can see who you are talking too. That's just a small additional touch that can help you get over the lack of in person contact.

Nutritional counseling is another revenue stream you may want to include in your business. You'll find that the 80/20 rule, or maybe even more likely, the 90/10 rule, applies in fitness and fat loss as well. Most people think that exercise is the best way to lose fat. Not true. It's one of the worst. The common perception is that if you start exercising, body fat will melt off like butter. The truth is that exercise can build muscle and raise metabolism, but in terms of burning the required calories to lose a significant amount of fat, it falls really short. As a result, fat loss tends to be about 10% exercise and 90% calorie control and appropriate nutritional prescription. This can be good for us as trainers because we already offer the exercise component, and most people are looking to lose some significant amount of body fat. So this presents an opportunity for an upsell into a nutritional counseling program too. You'll want to make sure that your state doesn't have further restrictions on nutritional information and coaching you can offer. Registered dietitians are licensed by the state and have a minimum level of education in order to provide their service. Be sure that you use the appropriate terminology and don't overstep the scope of your training. A great registered dietitian created software to help you implement this is the Diet master Pro web software from www.lifestylestech.com.

Metabolic testing is a service you can provide if you have the right equipment. It can be costly up front, but a crucial piece of information clients may need to know. If they suspect their metabolism is slow or not working how it should, you can find out in a reasonably accurate way buy using a tool called an indirect calorimeter. Microlife USA sells them in 2 product models. www.mimhs.com/home. The device can be costly up front, but also the mouth pieces which are disposable have to be continually purchased. However, you can provide a simple 8-10 minute reasonably accurate test for $50-$75 in addition to a client's regular training program with you. You can tell clients to keep their mouth piece and save it in a clean place for reuse on future tests. If they do this, you can offer them a discount instead of the full price for each succeeding test. The testing devices have been featured on The Biggest Loser TV show and have been used in several clinical trials. If you're skeptical of the accuracy, you'll also find the validation studies on Microlife's website.

Supplements are a very tricky area. Some people are 100% in favor of them. Others would never recommend them. Again, you can use your own discretion in this revenue stream. I like to have a source for quality fish oil, meal replacement drinks, and maybe a type of protein powder. Especially the meal replacement drinks for people who have trouble eating breakfast in the morning or tend to blow through the day without stopping to eat. If you choose to implement a revenue stream like this, the challenge is finding a reputable company as none of these products are evaluated or regulated by the FDA. That being said, we've been affiliated with Prograde www.getprograde.com for several years now and I have no complaints. It took about 3 years to find something I was willing to stake our reputation on and I still feel the same way today. You can also private label your own supplement line as well as other collateral. Again, I have heard no complaints about Private Label Fitness. All you have to do is send them your logo to place on their product and you can sell the products as your own brand. Pretty cool! Go to www.privatelabelfitness.com to get started.

DVD sales. We've all seen the fitness videos that have come and gone in our market. You can produce your own videos for sale too. And these days with the availability of cameras on our smart phones, Youtube, and the internet, we have easy access to producing these kinds of things on our own. Here's a great resource for making as few DVD's or as many as you want. www.kunaki.com. It's important to realize that Kunaki operates like an internet machine. It replicates what you have exactly. It is not a service. There isn't someone to call to talk about your needs. On the one hand that's good because you can spend as little as $1, but you've got to get it right and do it by yourself. It's really simple and should be a great resource for you especially starting out on a small scale.

Book or eBook sales are another excellent way for you to position yourself as the expert and open up another revenue stream in the process. Producing an eBook can be done very quickly and efficiently for next to nothing. Better still is that they are an infinite supply. You'll never run out of inventory and you can continue to resell at the same price. eBooks can be long and thorough or just in the form of a short report. They can be attached to or packaged in with other bonus items for higher price or used as a value add on. They don't even have to be attached to another electronic item, you can sell a copy of your eBook with the purchase of a personal training or nutritional package from you. Or couple it with the purchase of one of your branded clothing items.

Which leads me to the next point. Apparel sales. This may not be a huge portion of your revenue, but it can be a great add on especially concerning your loyal customers. Encourage them to purchase your branded apparel with your name and logo on it and wear it to the gym while working out with you or anywhere in public for that matter. A simple and easy resource to establish a basic line of branded apparel is Café Press. www.cafepress.com. Another easy one is Zazzle. www.zazzle.com. There isn't a huge profit margin here on things like this, but there are no up-front costs for you either. You just get paid the difference in the "wholesale price" you get from the website and the price point you sell it at. Café Press offers you your own "shop" online through which clients and other customers can purchase your branded apparel. This won't be the bulk of your business likely, but perhaps the increase in name recognition and visibility of you and your business could pay big dividends.

The sales of manuals can be in the form of more electronic offerings such as eBooks like we talked about earlier. Or, these can be hard copy printed materials. Perhaps something you sell along with your nutritional counseling program as a deliverable. A step by step manual for clients to take home and follow when they are not with you in person. You might have a client manual that you give to clients when they sign up that more thoroughly explains your philosophy, what they can expect, what to do when they are not with you, etc. Again, this can be added on as a deliverable for signing up. It always helps to add something tangible you can hand to a client after they write you a big check or put a large sum on their credit cards. This in combination with other value add ons and/or bonuses can increase the price of the initial sale you make.

And don't forget that is isn't all about you and your local market. You can offer things of value back to the industry itself. Just as I am doing here and with our numerous other fitness business tools and services, you can offer B2B (business to business) items. Let's say you've come up with a new advancement in the field. This is rare lately. There are a lot of junky trends out there, but I mean a real, legitimate advancement in the industry. It doesn't have to be anything Earth shattering, but just something that you came up with creatively that could be of benefit to all of us outside of your business. Be careful not to give away proprietary secrets that give you a competitive advantage. You'll have to make that decision. But, perhaps others might like to learn about your special methods. In this case, you could produce a special certification or a continuing education course for others in the industry to learn and for you to profit from. There's no sense in learning this wealth of knowledge if it is going to die with you. Sharing that kind of information, and you being justly and nicely compensated for it, is the kind of thing that will continue to drive progress. Check with some of the larger certification bodies like ACE American Council on Exercise to become a continuing education provider. You can produce programs others can take either in person or even that are web based. You'll have to pay an initial small fee to become a provider, but you'll get access to their entire network of certified professionals as potential customers of your educational materials.

Along the same lines of B2B offerings, consulting with other businesses after you've built up a good amount of experience and expertise, can be a VERY lucrative revenue stream. At any time, there is probably a business owner whose biggest problem is something that you have mastered. You could specialize in helping certain businesses do something difficult in which you've now become specialized. Again, this could be things along educational lines, maybe training other's staff that you are not directly in competition with. It could be certain methodologies, it could be setting up particular business systems, it could be specific marketing techniques, it could be a proprietary and proven sales system. There are limitless options here, but someone is likely to be in need of something you've become good at at any given time. And you can capitalize on that by consulting for them and giving them your expertise.

Mentoring can also take many forms. Most likely it might be in the form of interns you might take on from your local colleges and universities around you. Definitely don't discount that as a potential stream of new hire talent. If you mentor them through the internship process, they can be well trained prospective new hires ready to go as soon as the internship is over. And this doesn't always have to occur through an academic institution. If you've been successful, built up some good experience and become a well-respected trainer, you can choose to mentor other people in the field for a fee.

Software isn't something most trainers might think about producing, but it is a wide open area for us as most in fitness seem to be a little wary, if not outright afraid of, technology. Maybe you come up with a new online training technology. Maybe you design an app for smart phones or tablets. Maybe you come up with some kind of assessment software. We put an online fitness assessment on our website that we use for prospective clients to take themselves and opt into our email list. We've made that web code and directions for installation for sale in our store. Think about what you can do or who you can partner with to produce something in our industry using the technology that we have available to us. If you don't have a lot of money to pay someone to do the technical work up front, you could always try to partner with someone or have them consult for you using a revenue sharing model.

Let's talk about equipment. As a trainer, you'll likely be looked to as an expert on every piece of equipment on the market that comes along. Clients and friends will often ask you "What do you think about XYZ equipment?" That presents an opportunity for you to make recommendations that you can profit from or outright sales of your own equipment. The easiest way to profit from this is to participate in a drop shipping or affiliate program like the one from www.net2mallsdropship.com. It's very easy. They may not have everything you want, but it can be a good place to start or an additional avenue. All you need to do is set up an account and place the company's products on your site at a price point of your choosing above their wholesale price. Just like Café Press. When the customer buys from you at the retail price, you purchase the product from the company and input the customer's shipping address. You pocket the difference and the company fulfills the product shipment and customer service. That way you don't have to store and keep track of inventory. You're only brokering the sale of the product and keeping the marginal difference. It can't get any easier than that. There's no fees or up-front costs for you at all. It's just pure profit in the difference in price.

If you choose to set up a Wordpress blog/website, there are a myriad of plug in options available to you to customize the scope of what your website will do. One of the best ones I think is Wishlist Member membership site software.

You can download at www.member.wishlistproducts.com. There may be some less functional free options, but this one is rather inexpensive for what it does. You can completely customize for hidden membership content at multiple levels as much as you want. There is even a pay per post feature. You may be able to create a paid community within your website for existing clients where you hide special member/client only information and access or open up other levels to people from anywhere to access special content you contribute for a fee. It can be short term, longer term, or even open ended membership levels.

Joint ventures and co-promotion. You don't always have do all the work yourself. Someone else or another company may have the product or expertise that is a good complement to you or your company's mission. The simplest thing you can do is have a circle of friends who are not directly competing, but similar in nature who help share and promote each other's products and services. Let's say when you do a promotion, your massage therapist friend also shares your promotion with their network. And you do the same for them vice versa. We've done this before and a good way to go about it is to exchange gift cards. It costs you nothing other than for the cards themselves, but it is something of value you each can give out to your clients. There are many ways you can organize relationships like this. Just try to make sure it's as equitable as possible. You don't want one party doing all the promotion for someone else and not getting anything in return. You could take a more formal approach and engage in a true joint venture. This is a little more involved and can be problematic, but also a huge pay off. Companies do it all the time. You'll take your company and someone else's and create a third and separate venture that you both own and run together. It will likely require a new legal and tax entity, bank account, and compensation structure. The roles and responsibilities will have to be clearly defined or else the relationship runs the risk of falling apart. Another easy thing to do is affiliate sales. There are all kinds of affiliate programs and networks out there. Check out Amazon, Share a sale, Google affiliate network, and Clickbank www.clickbank.com for one of the biggest affiliate networks online. Clickbank is a little difficult to use as a vendor, but as an affiliate, it couldn't be any easier. It's mostly for electronic information type products and many of the vendors offer as much as 75% commission. That's the highest payout I've seen. Contrast that with an Amazon associate account's payout of 4-6% and you can see it's a pretty good deal. And you didn't have to create anything yourself. Let's say you have a site about martial arts and an audience who is interested in that subject. You can create a Clickbank account for free as an affiliate and promote one of the martial arts products. When you make a sale, you can get up to 75% commission on that sale. How is this possible? Vendors that do that will likely have an upsell or some kind of recurring revenue model where they make up that money on the back end after you made the initial sale. The good thing here too is that you will also likely get a percentage of the recurring revenue although not as high, but it is recurring revenue for you too as long as that person stays a paying client of the vendor. And you did all of this off of one sale. The challenging part of being an affiliate is getting enough traffic, either organically or through pay per click ads, to your affiliate links to convert to sales.

Special events, especially when tied in with something charitable or to support a local non-profit, can be a real valuable addition in terms of revenue streams. You might think, how is it possible to make more revenue when it's supposed to be for a non-profit or charity? It might not be immediately. It might be value in terms of the contact list of people you get who attend the event that you can later market to. Or, it might be revenue for you, but non-profits or charities available on hand to take additional donations. Or maybe a portion of your proceeds from the event will go to the non-profit or charities.

Sponsorships. You'll read more in a second about advertising in your facility, but right along with that, you could have local companies sponsor you or your company in exchange for placing their marketing collateral in view of your audience. Check with the other small businesses in your local area in addition to the larger companies. They may not be able to offer cash outright, but may be able to offer other things you need through in-kind donations and such. If your business' mission is a worthy cause, businesses will likely be more generous with their cash and expect little in return other than to help further the cause even though you are running a for profit venture. Of course, you can always offer them discounted or free training too as an exchange. If you do it right, and have multiple levels of sponsorship, you might even make a profit. Think about that. If you can cover all of your overhead with sponsorships, that leaves a lot of room and cash for you to do other things you'd like to do.

Advertising directly in your facility. If your facility or

location outside gets enough traffic flowing through it and is the right audience for other companies in your area, you can sell advertising space. Many of my business associates will hang large banners from local companies inside of their facilities in exchange for an advertising fee. Maybe you can place advertising in your front windows, lobby area, website, newsletter, or even your uniform that your clientele will see.

CONCLUSION

I've thoroughly enjoyed writing this book and I think it will be an invaluable resource for many existing trainers and businesses as well as those that would like to get started on an entrepreneurial journey in fitness. I hope you get something out of these tools and principles we've put together for you. There is more to come from us at S.P.A.R.T.A. Be sure to see the additional personal trainer resources at the end of this section.

Additional Personal Trainer Resources

S.P.A.R.T.A. blog www.spartatraining.com/blog - Bringing professionalism to the fitness industry.

S.P.A.R.T.A. store www.spartatraining.com/store - Personal trainer business tools and services.

Droodly www.droodly.com – Sell advertising space on your site through an auction format.

Dropbox www.dropbox.com - Save files in web space for back up or use on other devices like other computers you have or your mobile. Even share files with others like your employees.

Screenr www.screenr.com - Free and instant screencasts. Just click record. Plays everywhere for your audience to view and is sharable over social media. No downloads or installing either.

Ning www.ning.com - Create more of a sense of community by creating your own social network. Do it for free or make it exclusive or for paying members only.

Google Scholar ww.scholar.google.com – A great resource for looking up scholarly research articles in the health and fitness industry.

ABOUT THE AUTHOR

Chris Lutz, Owner and Master Trainer

Chris Lutz is the owner and founder of S.P.A.R.T.A. He has a degree from George Mason University in Exercise Science and has over a decade of professional experience as a certified personal trainer. Teaching, reading and writing about proper exercise methodology are his biggest passions. Chris and his team can properly teach you how to obtain a full body workout in 30 minutes, 2-3 times per week using a safe, effective and efficient method called high intensity training.

Experience

Chris has worked as a personal trainer since 1999. He got his start at a Fairfax, VA fitness club where he instructed in a one-on-one high intensity personal training facility, conducted client health assessments, recorded fitness improvement, instructed members in proper circuit weight training (high intensity training), and oversaw fellow fitness center employees. In 2001, Chris was the manager and head instructor at a Sterling, VA High Intensity Training (HIT) facility. He developed both the general and post-rehabilitative strength training programs, evaluated client health histories, conducted follow-up fitness assessments, communicated with and maintained the club's 275 clients, participated in the hiring and training of employees, and managed all facility administrative duties. His previous work history, combined with his knowledge, expertise, and passion for fitness allowed him to successfully open S.P.A.R.T.A. in 2007.

Education

National Strength Professionals Association (NSPA)
Certified Personal Trainer

George Mason University

Bachelor of Science: Exercise Science, High-Intensity Training
Health, Fitness, and Recreation Resources Dept.
Fairfax, VA
2000 – 2004

Chris' combination of B.S. degree, high intensity training CPT certification, and over 5 years experience managing a training facility, earned him his Master Trainer status.

Related Collegiate Activities
GMU Ice Hockey Team Assistant Captain

Outside Interests
Reading scientific and philosophical periodicals and books. Writing persuasive and/or educational articles. Outdoor sports such as camping, kayaking/canoeing, fishing, and hunting. Skating and playing ice hockey.

Printed in Great Britain
by Amazon.co.uk, Ltd.,
Marston Gate.